HANG THE DJ?

The Radio Presenter's Guide to the Law

**Paul Hollins
and Paul Chantler**

Foreword by Simon Bates

Dedication from Paul Hollins

To my family and friends
whose support has never ceased to amaze me.

Dedication from Paul Chantler

To my beloved and much-missed dad,
Peter Victor Chantler, 1929-2010

Contents

.

Part 2: CONTEMPT OF COURT – The Right to a Fair Trial

Acknowledgments

The authors would like to offer their thanks and acknowledgments to the following:

Francis Currie, International Radio Consultant

James Rea, Head of News at Global Radio

Peter Stewart, BBC

John Pickford, Key 103

Simon Bates, Smooth Radio

Morrissey and Marr, whose lyrics inspired the title

All the people whose stories are featured

Foreword

 "Tell him he can go stuff himself," said my large and amiable boss in an Australian radio station. He was on the phone to a solicitor — and I was in trouble.

I had recounted on air a lurid story about a well known, buyable and universally disliked politician. I'd been at an event and had reported what I had observed to be accurate in what I thought was a pretty hilarious tale. It was entertaining radio and true. Well, more or less.

The politician, his family and his lawyers erupted. A standard letter arrived after a contentious phone call.

My boss was generally supportive: "You stupid bugger, what did you go and say that for? It's bloody libellous and you know it. I'm going to have to pull a few favours on this — and that'll bugger up my drinking time."

But these were different days in a far-away place. Comments could be denied — and they were; off air recordings could go missing — and they did.

Politicians knew to keep the media sweet otherwise their wrongdoings would spill out in a dozen different ways.

Those were the days things could be fixed amicably and privately between the parties. That one went away.

Fast forward many years — leaping smartly over Kenny Everett being fired from the BBC for making a fairly innocuous comment about the then Minister of Transport and many of the stories told in this book — to the recent past and a comment made by yours truly.

"So and so," I opined of a well known politician, "is little more than a publicity seeking opportunist". And he was — but again, that isn't the point.

The solicitors' letter was in my hands within thirty minutes. I called my own splendid solicitor. "We have a problem", she said.

"Don't be silly, that's fair comment", say I blithely.

"Well, that's a good argument," she said. "But all he wants is five hundred quid and if we even take it to the steps of the court, it's going to cost you five times that in my fees".

Hmmm. We settled. And yes, I know that I was wrong so to do, but I plead overwork at the time and a fear of dentists and the High Court.

My point is that we all, as broadcasters, sail effortlessly into choppy legal waters every day on air. We do our best to be professional and balanced, to be fair and honest in our dealings with life and not to get ourselves into a legal tangle.

But, even if you've been in the business for years, you still need to be reminded of the horrors that could await you and of the quicksand that could open and swallow you after an unguarded word or five.

At the very least, this fascinating book by Paul Hollins and Paul Chantler has a thrill — or maybe a shudder — on every page. And it just might serve as a saviour the next time you're tired and tempted to go one step beyond.

Simon Bates
London, July 2011

Introduction

The intention of this book is to give you a general overview of the laws of defamation and contempt, and how it can affect what you do on the radio as well as what read out on air from social media sites such as Facebook and Twitter.

The stories included highlight the need for you to be fully aware and have an understanding of defamation and contempt laws so you can broadcast confidently. By showing you real-life example stories it may help you to avoid similar situations.

This book isn't about scaremongering or making you worry unnecessarily, it's simply about helping reduce the risk of finding yourself and your radio station at the centre of very expensive legal action.

Please note that the content is based on the legal system of England and Wales. It may differ in other countries and jurisdictions, so please be sure to check.

Furthermore laws can — and do — change, so if you are a broadcaster please make sure you stay fully up-to-date with any changes.

Paul Hollins
London, July 2011

Part 1

DEFAMATION

. . .

Protecting Reputations

What Is Defamation?

The word defamation literally means to "de-fame" someone. In other words, harming their reputation or good name.

The law says everyone has a right to a good name throughout their lives, unless there is undeniable evidence to the contrary such as being convicted of a crime.

Defamation is divided into two parts — Libel and Slander.

> LIBEL is written defamation in a newspaper, book, magazine, website, social media network — or broadcast on radio or television.

> SLANDER is spoken defamation. Anyone suing for slander has to prove an actual loss or damage, for example that someone has lost money or their job.

Despite radio speech being spoken, it's considered to be libel rather than slander because it's effectively 'published' to a large number of people through transmission.

What Is Libel?

Libel is anything published or broadcast which:

> Exposes someone to HATRED, RIDICULE, CONTEMPT or DISGRACE.

> Leads someone to be SHUNNED or AVOIDED.

> Injures someone in their BUSINESS, OFFICE, TRADE or PROFESSION.

> Lowers someone in the eyes of "right-thinking members of society generally".

.

What Is the Purpose of Libel Law?

Libel law protects individuals and organisations from unwarranted, mistaken or untruthful attacks on their reputation.

If you are libelled you are entitled to launch a case against the person or company who libelled you.

For example, in 2002 rights campaigner Victoria Gillick won a £5,000 settlement and an apology after taking libel action against a sexual health charity.

The charity alleged that Mrs Gillick was responsible for a rise in teenage pregnancies. The case went to court as Mrs Gillick believed she had been libelled by the Brook charity.

On the next page you can see how her council successfully argued that she had indeed been libelled and how she was subsequently awarded damages and an apology.

Victoria Gillick Case

BBC NEWS

Thursday, 12 December, 2002, 11:32 GMT

Morals campaigner wins damages

The case was heard at the High Court

Morals campaigner Victoria Gillick has won an apology and £5,000 damages in a libel case against a teenage sexual health advice charity.

Mrs Gillick claimed the Brook charity, which offers advice on contraception and sexual health, libelled her in a 1996 fact sheet 'Teenage Conceptions: Statistics and Trends'.

In it, the charity alleged Mrs Gillick's 1983 challenge against the legality of government guidelines on contraception advice for under 16s, was one of the reasons for a rise in teenage conceptions during the 1980s

The mother of 10 from Wisbech, Cambridgeshire, claimed Brook Advisory Centres and their former chief executive Dr Margaret Jones libelled her in the fact-sheet.

Mrs Gillick was challenging a previous High Court judgement which found in Brook's favour.

> 66 Brook have never accepted that the fact sheet does libel Mrs Gillick in the way she alleges 99
>
> Tamsin Allen, Brook

She said after the appeal hearing: "The damages have always been irrelevant.

"I'm delighted and relieved that not only has my name been cleared but the truth has been allowed to come out."

'Moral blame'

Mrs Gillick's solicitor-advocate David Price told Mr Justice Eady at the High Court: "This statement caused Mrs Gillick considerable concern and distress.

"She understood the words to mean that, by her court action, she was morally responsible for the rise in teenage conception.

"Mrs Gillick denies that her legal action led to an increase in teenage conception let alone that she could bear any moral blame for such a rise."

Brook agreed to apologise for the words in the fact sheet, he said.

"They acknowledge unreservedly that any suggestion that Mrs Gillick bore a moral responsibility for an increase in pregnancies among 15-19 year olds during the 1980s is without foundation and apologise to Mrs Gillick for this distress caused to her."

Tamsin Allen, for Brook, which has also agreed to pay Mrs Gillick's legal costs bills, said it had not intended to allege Mrs Gillick was morally responsible for an increase in pregnancies, and "regretted" the fact sheet could be interpreted in that way.

She said: "Brook have never accepted that the fact sheet does libel Mrs Gillick in the way she alleges and the parties have agreed to disagree on that issue."

The Victoria Gillick case highlights why Libel Laws exist. Mrs Gillick successfully brought action again the Brook charity for alleging she bore a responsibility for a rise in teenage pregnancies during the 1980s.

Source: BBC Website
http://news.bbc.co.uk/1/hi/health/2569063.stm

How Does Libel Affect Radio?

When you're on-air you have the power to influence and that comes with huge responsibility.

As a presenter, it's vitally important that you are aware of your legal obligations because the consequences of getting it wrong can be incredibly severe.

A lack of knowledge is no defence.

Although most libel cases appear to be brought against newspapers, it doesn't mean that radio stations and radio presenters are exempt.

A slip of the tongue can result in a libel lawsuit.

Libel is all about the meaning of words or phrases and what a reasonable person understands and thinks about them. This takes into account inference, implication and innuendo.

If you do ever say something libellous, then the person or company you have defamed has the right to launch legal proceedings against you personally as well as the radio station.

It's worth remembering that it's not just famous people who sue for libel. Anyone can bring legal proceedings if they believe they have a case. We'll touch on this more later in the book.

By law all radio stations have to keep a recorded 'log' of their output for 42 days. This means if a libel comment is broadcast, then the station will have a copy of it. Chances are you will need to provide this recording in court so an overview of context can be considered.

"Allegedly" Won't Protect You

The long-running satirical TV comedy programme *Have I Got News For You* has made a running joke of saying things about people prefixed by the word "allegedly".

This has led to a generation of radio presenters thinking that if they prefix or suffix what they say with "allegedly", then it will cover them against legal action.

It won't.

In fact, if a case is brought against you it could actually harm your defence as by using "allegedly" it shows you were aware the subject matter was potentially malicious and/or libellous.

Why 'Comedy' Is No Defence

TV comedy shows are cleverly edited to give the impression that 'anything goes' and the participants can say whatever they want.

In reality, the content of these shows is screened by a professional team of lawyers ahead of transmission to ensure anything broadcast stays well within acceptable boundaries. This is because the producer wants to create an entertainment show, not get sued.

When you're on-air remember that a joke or throw-away comment can easily be libellous.

MP George Galloway successfully sued for libel against a small Jewish radio station that implied he was anti-Semitic. The comments involved a spoof character called 'Georgie Galloway'.

Despite an on-air apology, an apology on the station's website and the DJ in question being fired, Mr Galloway was still awarded £15,000. The station had to close down as a result of the costs.

Even if you make it clear that a comment you make is a joke, it can still get you into trouble.

A highly-experienced presenter on a station in the North of England read out an email in 2005 from a listener inquiring about someone who used to be on air on that station some years before.

The presenter named the person and said: "He's alright. He's just come out of prison. The kiddy fiddling charges were dropped." He laughed as he quickly added; "only joking of course!"

The radio station was sued for libel by the person referred to — and had to pay damages of several thousand pounds and broadcast an apology.

George Galloway Case

THE INDEPENDENT

London's Jewish radio station closes after Galloway sues

By Michael Savage
Tuesday, 12 August 2008

London's only Jewish community radio station has been forced to cease broadcasting after losing a High Court libel case brought against it by the Respect MP George Galloway.

Jcom, a non-profit station which broadcast online and to a small area in north-west London, was wound up after it was told to pay the MP damages of £15,000.

Mr Galloway sued the station after one of its presenters played a spoof character based on the MP for Bethnal Green and Bow, and implied he was anti-Semitic. It was also ordered to pay Mr Galloway's court costs, thought to be £5,000. Mr Galloway said that the judgment had "categorically crushed the slur of anti-Semitism".

During a broadcast in November, a presenter who called himself "Georgie Galloway", the station's "Middle East correspondent", used the catchphrase, "kill the Jews, kill the Jews". The station immediately sacked the presenter, Richard Malach, saying he was "young and inexperienced" and had made an error of judgment while attempting to present an edgy programme. It also issued an apology on its website and offered Mr Galloway the opportunity to appear on the station, which had a very small audience. Only 36 people were listening online at the time of the offending show.

The programme was also broadcast over the radio to an area in north-west London with a three-mile radius.

But Mr Galloway said he pursued the case as the station's apology "fell short of the categorical retraction of the imputation of anti-Semitism that I insisted upon".

Jeremy Silverstone, the head of Jcom, said he was disappointed that the case had led to the downfall of the capital's only Jewish radio station.

Respect MP George Galloway took action against a small Jewish community radio station who he claimed had libelled him. Although the station took swift action, the cost of damages and associated legal fees resulted in the closure of station.

Source: Independent Newspaper Website
http://www.independent.co.uk/news/uk/home-news/londons-jewish-radio-station-closes-after-galloway-sues-891492.html

Repeating a Libel
Is Just as Bad

Did you know that simply repeating a libel is enough for someone to take legal action against you?

In the eyes of the law, it doesn't matter if you're quoting from another source; if you repeat a libel you are as much to blame for publishing it as the original source.

Always exercise EXTREME CARE when using a newspaper story or even the internet as a source.

The concern here is that a potentially libellous showbiz story could be picked up by a presenter and used as a 'showbiz bit'. By using that story on-air you too could face action as you have effectively repeated it.

The breakfast show team at a radio station in the South of England once read an item from a tabloid newspaper in their 'showbiz news' slot, referring to the marital problems of a famous comedian.

The comedian in question lived in the radio station's area, heard the item — and successfully sued both the newspaper and radio station as the information was untrue.

There are many instances where celebrities have taken legal action over stories that were found to be untrue, as you'll see from the following examples.

Ozzy Osborne Case

June 5, 2008 11:29

FIRST FOR MUSIC NEWS

Ozzy Osbourne wins libel damages from tabloid newspaper

Daily Star forced to pay out over false health-based claims

Ozzy Osbourne has been awarded libel damages from the **Daily Star** newspaper after the newspaper falsely accused him of having a health scare that jeopardised this year's **Brit Awards**, which he co-presented.

The newspaper wrongly claimed that **Osbourne** collapsed twice before the awards ceremony, which took place in **Earl's Court** in **London** in February.

The ruling was made in the **London High Court**, although **Osbourne** was not present to hear it.

The singer has indicated that the damages, the amount of which was undisclosed, will be donated to his wife **Sharon Osbourne**'s colon cancer charity.

The original story which appeared in the Daily Star had wrongly claimed that Ozzy Osborne had suffered a health scare ahead of the 2008 Brit Awards. Had this story been repeated by a presenter/radio station, they too could've faced legal action.

Source: NME Magazine Website
http://www.nme.com/news/ozzy-osbourne/37115

Kate Winslet Case

BBC NEWS

Page last updated at 11:08 GMT, Tuesday, 3 November 2009

✉ E-mail this to a friend   🖨 Printable version

Kate Winslet accepts libel payout

Oscar-winning actress Kate Winslet has accepted £25,000 libel damages over a claim made by the Daily Mail that she lied about her exercise regime.

The settlement was agreed at London's High Court on Tuesday, but the actress was not present for the hearing.

Kate Winslet won an Oscar for her role in The Reader

In May, the 34-year-old filed legal papers saying she was "distressed and embarrassed" by the feature.

In a statement the actress said: "I am delighted that the Mail have apologised for making false allegations about me."

She added: "I was particularly upset to be accused of lying about my exercise regime and felt that I had a responsibility to request an apology in order to demonstrate my commitment to the views that I have always expressed about body issues, including diet and exercise.

"I strongly believe that women should be encouraged to accept themselves as they are, so to suggest that I was lying was an unacceptable accusation of hypocrisy."

'Irritating actress'

The star, who won an Oscar for The Reader, said the claims injured her personal and professional reputation.

The offending article, headlined "Should Kate Winslet win an Oscar for the world's most irritating actress?" was printed in January.

Her solicitor, Rachel Atkins, told Mr Justice Eady the feature was accompanied by several naked photographs of the actress in various films and was offensive in tone.

"The claimant has frequently asserted the right of women to accept the way that they look and by accusing her of trying to mislead the public, the defendant caused her a great deal of distress. It was simply not true," Ms Atkins said.

The newspaper published an apology in September, accepting that Winslet had not lied about how much she exercised, and agreed to pay the damages and costs.

The article disputed a quote given to Elle magazine, in which Winslet said: "I don't go to the gym because I don't have time, but I do Pilates workout DVDs for 20 minutes or more every day at home."

In 2007, Winslet accepted an undisclosed settlement from Grazia magazine over allegations that she had visited a diet doctor.

The publication apologised and accepted that Winslet had visited a doctor to be treated for a neck problem.

The Daily Mail had printed a story that wrongly claimed Kate Winslet had lied about her exercise regime. The story was later proved to be false and Ms. Winslet won damages for libel from the newspaper. Any station that had repeated the earlier story could have faced action.

Source: BBC Website
http://news.bbc.co.uk/1/hi/entertainment/8339830.stm

Nicole Kidman Case #1

BBC NEWS

Last Updated: Friday, 14 December 2007, 12:48 GMT

✉ E-mail this to a friend   🖨 Printable version

Kidman wins damages in scent row

Actress and Chanel spokeswoman Nicole Kidman has won an apology from the UK's Daily Telegraph after the paper claimed she promoted a rival brand of perfume.

The Oscar-winning star, 40, will receive undisclosed damages over allegations that she used a non-Chanel scent during a recent visit to London.

Kidman signed a deal to promote fashion house Chanel in 2003

Kidman's solicitor John Kelly said she had suffered considerable embarrassment and distress over the story.

The star was not at London's High Court for the settlement of her libel action.

Mr Kelly said Kidman intended to donate her "substantial" damages to Unifem, the United Nations Development Fund for Women.

Premiere

In an item published in its Spy gossip column last month, the Telegraph alleged Kidman had upset Chanel by using Jo Malone perfume while promoting her latest film in London.

She was attending the premiere of The Golden Compass, a fantasy production based on the fiction of British author Philip Pullman.

Mr Kelly said the story wrongly suggested Kidman had acted in an unprofessional and disloyal manner and had flouted her contractual obligations.

David Price, representing the Daily Telegraph, said the paper "accepts the allegations are untrue and ought never to have been published".

Actress Nicole Kidman successfully won damages from the Daily Telegraph who had wrongly alleged she promoted a rival brand of perfume while contracted to Chanel. The story was said to have caused embarrassment and distress and, as a result, Ms. Kidman won substantial damages. If a station had repeated the earlier story, they too could've been named in the lawsuit.

Source: BBC Website
http://news.bbc.co.uk/1/hi/entertainment/7144331.stm

The Burden of Proof Lies with the Defendant

Almost uniquely in English law, in libel cases the burden of proof lies with the author / publisher and not the complainant. In other words, you have to prove that what you write or say is true. The person you have targeted does not have to prove that you are wrong.

For example, if you called someone "a junkie" on-air and they took action against you (and the radio station), it is up to you to be able to prove in court that they ARE on drugs. The defendant doesn't have to prove that they are not on drugs. This is a key distinction. It's highly important that you understand this.

One of the most effective ways to protect yourself against the threat of libel is to only ever use verifiable facts. A verifiable fact is one that is capable of being proven true or false. So, ask yourself:

> Is it true?

> Can you prove it?

> Would you like this said about you?

In 2002 actor and singer Jimmy Nail launched proceedings when it was wrongly claimed that he had been 'demanding' during the filming of a TV drama.

A radio presenter — who also had a column in a local newspaper — made an error of judgement and used this material both on-air and in her newspaper column.

Mr Nail launched legal proceedings and because the burden of proof lies with the person who made the claims, Mr Nail was able to successfully win damages.

Remember, if you libel someone it's you who has to prove that you are justified in making that claim. The person who has been libelled doesn't have to deny anything.

Jimmy Nail Case

Monday, 16 December, 2002, 14:41 GMT

Actor Nail wins libel payout

Jimmy Nail was accused of throwing a "showbiz strop"

Jimmy Nail, one of the stars of Auf Wiedersehen Pet, has won undisclosed damages from newspaper publishers after they ran stories claiming he had been difficult and demanding during filming.

Newcastle Chronicle and Journal Ltd, the publishers of the Sunday Sun, and columnist Karen Wight have agreed to pay the star damages after a statement was read in the High Court on Monday morning.

Manuel Barca, the counsel for the publishers and Ms Wight, apologised on behalf of his clients for causing Mr Nail any distress or embarrassment.

Mr Nail was not present in court, but his solicitor, Martin Cruddace, told Mr Justice Morland at the court on Monday the allegations were made in Karen Wight's gossip column in the Sunday Sun newspaper.

In the article Wight alleged the star had insisted he be moved to a more luxurious hotel than the rest of the cast while filming the show's recent episodes.

There were also claims that Mr Nail had refused to attend a press launch in his home town, Newcastle, because he was not being paid an appearance fee.

The allegations were also printed on the paper's website.

Ms Wight was also said to have "dished the dirt" on the star's "rude" behaviour during her show on the city's Galaxy 105 radio station.

Mr Cruddace said: "Newcastle Chronicle and Journal Ltd and Ms Wight accepted that all the allegations were totally untrue and without any substance whatsoever.

The programme saw the old crew reunited in America

"The actor did attend the press launch in Newcastle and neither requested or received an appearance fee.

"As such, the publication of the allegations had caused grave damage to his personal and professional reputation and he had suffered considerable embarrassment and distress.

"This was particularly acute given the timing of the publication to coincide with the new series."

Popularity

Mr Cruddace added that the suggestion Nail had "forgotten" his roots was particularly upsetting as he was "extremely proud" of his background.

The actor had always "championed the North East and striven to bring business and work to the area", he said.

Mr Nail, who plays Oz in the series, took part in the reunion episode, the first new episode of the show in 15 years.

The programme saw the British builders trying to build a bridge in Arizona.

The BBC is considering making another series of the show after the popularity of this year's episodes.

More than 12 million people tuned in to the first episode of the new show when it aired in May, and the series won best comedy drama at Saturday's comedy awards.

Jimmy Nail successfully won damages regarding a wrongful claim that he was demanding during the filming of a TV drama. This story underlines the fact that if you are making a statement about someone, it is imperative that you only use verifiable facts and not just hearsay.

Source: BBC Website
http://news.bbc.co.uk/1/hi/entertainment/showbiz/2579871.stm

Is 'Honest Comment' a Defence?

The law allows people to have honestly-held opinions.

An honestly held opinion is not libellous in itself as long as the opinion is not malicious, derogatory or could cause harm to someone's reputation.

For example if you attended a concert by a band and you thought the lead-singer's vocal performance was "rubbish", that's fine as it's your honestly held opinion.

However, if you also added "it was so bad people were walking out" then you could be sued unless you can prove in court that people were indeed walking out.

Remember it's up to you to prove it — not for the singer (or anyone else) to deny it.

The reason you could have action taken against you is that by adding the statement that "people were walking out," it may negatively influence someone else's opinion of the band and perhaps even cause financial harm to them if a person decides to seek a refund on their ticket rather than see them in concert.

You can criticise someone's performance — but to imply they weren't trying could be libellous.

You can't go over-the-top with criticism either.

The actress Charlotte Cornwall sued tabloid newspaper the Sunday People and its columnist Nina Myskow in 1985 for commenting about a theatre performance in her 'Wally of the Week' column: "She can't sing, her bum is too big and she has the sort of stage presence that jams lavatories."

She was awarded £11,000 damages because the judge said that criticism must not "pass out of the domain of criticism itself." In other words, critics can't make derogatory statements in the guise of criticism.

Celebs Are Fair Game Though, Right?

Wrong! It's a misnomer to think that just because someone chooses to be in the public eye that they are 'fair game' and that you can therefore say anything you like about them.

There are numerous examples of libel payouts when inaccurate stories about celebrities and their private lives have been splashed over the pages of a newspaper.

As we touched on earlier — and now seems a good place for a reminder — repeating a libel is just as bad as being the originator. If you run a 'Showbiz News' type feature or a 'gossip' segment, be EXTREMELY careful.

Here are more cases where celebrities have won damages over incorrect stories which, if repeated when first published, could have resulted in radio stations (and DJs) also being sued.

Nicole Kidman Case #2

 NEWS

Last Updated: Thursday, 31 July, 2003, 11:48 GMT 12:48 UK

✉ E-mail this to a friend   🖨 Printable version

Kidman wins libel case

Nicole Kidman has been awarded "substantial" undisclosed damages following newspaper suggestions that she had an adulterous affair with actor Jude Law.

Nicole Kidman was starring in The Hours when the story was printed

Kidman also accepted a public apology from the Daily Mail at the High Court.

A libel judge heard that the Daily Mail newspaper alleged she had led Law, who was married with young children, to cheat on his wife, causing the breakdown of his marriage.

It was also suggested in the article on 6 March that her repeated denials of the affair were dishonest.

"The publication of this article has caused grave damage to the claimant's personal and professional reputation and she has suffered considerable embarrassment and distress," solicitor Gideon Benaim told Mr Justice Gray.

"Her embarrassment was particularly acute as the allegations coincided with the run-up the Oscars award ceremony in Los Angeles in which she had been nominated for an award for Best Actress in a Leading Role for her role in The Hours."

Daily Mail editor Paul Dacre and journalist Nicole Lampert freely accepted that the allegations were untrue and without foundation.

They apologised for the distress and embarrassment caused and agreed to pay legal costs as well as damages.

Nicole Kidman brought libel proceedings against the Daily Mail newspaper after they suggested she had an affair. It's important to understand that if you repeat a libel like this, a claim can be brought against you too.

Source: BBC Website
http://news.bbc.co.uk/1/hi/entertainment/film/3113353.stm

Diana Rigg Case

BBC NEWS

Last Updated: Tuesday, 21 October, 2003, 09:04 GMT 10:04 UK

E-mail this to a friend   Printable version

Actress Rigg wins newspaper fight

Actress Dame Diana Rigg has won a £38,000 libel payout from two newspapers over stories calling her an "embittered woman" who was retiring from acting.

Avengers star Dame Diana, 65, took action after articles appeared in the Daily Mail and Evening Standard.

Dame Diana was in court to hear the settlement

She said the untrue claim that she had announced her retirement would harm her chances of working in the future.

And the report that she was bitter and "held British men in low regard" was also false, she said.

The Evening Standard and Daily Mail, both owned by Associated Newspapers, must also pay costs and will make a charity donation.

The contentious articles were published after Dame Diana gave an interview to promote the Children With Aids charity.

> 66 Dame Diana was upset at the portrayal of her which quite wrongly suggested that she is an embittered woman 99
>
> Tom Amlot
> Lawyer

The Daily Mail article, published in September 2002, was headlined: "Diana Rigg attacks British men and announces her retirement."

It implied that the whole interview was about her private life, which was not the case, and that she had talked about her first marriage and the break-up of her second marriage.

Professional reputation

Her lawyer Tom Amlot told the High Court in London: "Dame Diana was upset at the portrayal of her which quite wrongly suggested that she is an embittered woman and holds British men in low regard.

"She was also concerned that her professional reputation and ability to secure work would be damaged by the statement that she was retiring when she is not."

She is due to start rehearsals for the Tennessee Williams play Suddenly Last Summer in January.

Dame Diana became a 1960s icon as leather-clad spy Emma Peel in The Avengers, and also appeared in James Bond thriller On Her Majesty's Secret Service.

Actress Diana Rigg won damages after two newspapers made unsubstantiated claims about her. When the original story was run it could have easily been reiterated by a radio station, thus making them as liable as the newspapers.

Source: BBC Website
http://news.bbc.co.uk/1/hi/entertainment/showbiz/3210018.stm

Not Naming the Person Makes It OK?

Again, this is a popular misconception. The law states that if the person is identifiable then they can take legal action.

The word 'identifiable' is key as it means that even if you don't directly name the person, they can still launch legal proceedings against you if they can be easily identified from what you said or the way you described them.

If a person or group can establish that the offending words apply to them, they have a case.

For example, if you alluded to the fact that an author of a book regarding radio libel was having an affair then you're in as much danger of being sued as if you'd just come out and named them. Reason is you've pretty much identified them and a reasonable person could work out who you mean.

And remember, you can libel companies as well as individuals.

No One Famous Will Ever Know if I Libel Them

It's dangerous to think along those lines because even if you work in a very small marketplace, streaming and digital media now means you potentially have a much wider audience, so you never know who might be listening.

These days it's not just your local FM or AM transmission area you're broadcasting to.

Many famous people actually employ companies to monitor the media to ensure nothing defamatory or derogatory is being said or written about them.

It's worth remembering that the person who you've libelled (famous or not) doesn't actually need to have heard it with their own ears in order to take action. In fact they don't even need to have heard it at the time of transmission.

If they do make a legal complaint you may be required by law to supply a recording from your own 'logger'.

The point is… don't just assume that because you work in a smaller market that you won't be found out.

'Rumours' and 'Wicked Whispers' Are Risky

A comment can still be libellous even if it is reported as a rumour.

Worse still, it can also be libellous even if it is reported as being untrue.

For example, if you were to say something like, "There's a rumour going around that Frank at the corner-shop has been selling out-of-date food, but don't worry because the stuff I've bought there has always been fine" it could still be considered libellous.

This is because the 'rumour part' is based on a defamatory comment which you are effectively repeating.

Therefore if 'Frank' believes that because you mentioned this rumour exists that you are perpetuating it, he could claim that you are further damaging his name, reputation and trade; and as a result could take action against you.

If he were to do so, remember he is under no obligation to prove that he HASN'T been selling out of date food, but you may to have prove in court that he was because you repeated the libellous rumour.

Always take great care with how you approach rumours, so you don't put yourself at risk.

Take Care with Callers and Guests

If you take callers live to air or have guests in the studio or down the line, remember that something THEY say could be libellous too.

In a live situation, you're partially protected from being sued for libel by what's called the Live Defence — otherwise known legally as Innocent Dissemination.

This defence says that there's a legal protection if you were live on air, took all reasonable precautions to ensure a libel didn't happen, had no reason to suspect it would and had no effective control over the speaker.

Remember, though, it applies only to the guest or caller — not you or any other radio professional who are deemed to know better.

If you suspect a libel is happening live, you should stop your guest or caller (so they don't repeat the libel), offer an apology without repeating it yourself and make sure you distance the radio station from the comments.

This won't mean you 'get off' with the libel, but it will show the courts that you took immediate decisive action.

Always be on your guard and keep your wits about you, even in the most innocent of circumstances.

A presenter at a station in the South East of England was talking to an eight year old competition contestant on the phone in 1999. During the chat, the presenter asked about the child's school, his favourite subjects and favourite teacher. He also asked, "Who's the worst teacher in the school?"

It was obviously meant as a bit of fun — but by asking this question, the youngster named the teacher whose reputation suffered as a result.

The teacher — financially backed by her union — threatened to sue the station. An out-of-court settlement was eventually reached.

Killer Costs – and Saying Sorry

If you're sued for libel, the legal fees and payment of damages can run into thousands of pounds.

All radio stations have defamation insurance which covers the costs of fees and damages. However, like home or motor insurance, the premium paid rockets if the insurance is subject to a claim so libel can cost a station real cash.

It is possible — though unlikely — that someone suing a station for libel might also sue you as an individual.

As a radio presenter (whether freelance or employed) it may be worth considering 'Professional Indemnity Insurance' which would cover you in the unfortunate event of a legal case being taken against you.

Choose a reputable insurer and enquire about taking out a policy, especially if you are a breakfast or talk show host.

The other cost to consider, apart from the ones above, is that of personal impact. Being the subject of legal action puts huge pressure on an individual. And I mean that in a sense of financially, emotionally, professionally and so on.

Bear in mind that if a case were to be brought against you the radio station you currently work for may:

> Fire you for bringing yourself (and/or them) into disrepute

> Expect YOU to indemnify THEM against any costs they incur (i.e. you are responsible for any fines/damages levied against the station). Check your contract to see if this is the case (it usually is)

Any libel action also means an increase in paperwork and meetings for your bosses as they try to sort things out with the lawyers and insurers.

In addition to damages and costs, the settlement of a libel action usually requires an apology either read out in court or, from time to time, on air.

Apologies need careful wording so leave this to the lawyers and don't try to say sorry yourself without advice as it could get you into even more trouble.

Things You Should Avoid Saying and Doing On-Air

As a radio presenter you should always exercise care before opening the microphone, even if you're on a tightly formatted music station.

These are the types of things you should avoid, to help ensure you don't find yourself in hot water.

> Accusing people of crimes they have not committed

> Alleging they are incompetent

> Alleging they are a hypocrite

> Alleging they are obnoxious

> Alleging they are negligent

> Alleging they are dishonest or immoral

> Accusing them of sexual or financial impropriety

> Accusing them of lying

> Accusing them of doing disreputable deeds

The following is a list of 'Danger Words' — words you should be very cautious about using.

This list is by no means exhaustive but it will give you a good idea of the types of words you should always strive to avoid:

adulterous	hypocrite	rapist
bankrupt	immoral	retarded
bribery	incompetent	rip-off
compulsive liar	insane	satanic
communist	insolvent	scab
con	junkie	shyster
corrupt	liar	sleazebag
coward	mafia	slut
criminal	mentally diseased	snitch
crook	misappropriated funds	spy
drug addict	Nazi	stupid
drug dealer	odd-ball	swindling
evil	paranoid	thieving
fake	pervert	traitorous
fraud	pimp	unethical
fascist	plagiarist	unprofessional
gold-digger	prostitute	unscrupulous
like Hitler	queer	unsound
homosexual	racist	vile

It's a Matter of Context

There are times where you need to exercise a greater level of care when making a comment or describing a person in order to avoid libel.

For example it's fine to describe someone as 'all fingers and thumbs' in everyday life, however if you were using that adjective to describe a prominent neurosurgeon then it could be deemed libellous.

This is because the description you have used is derogatory.

A neurosurgeon naturally needs a steady hand, so being described as "all fingers and thumbs" leads to a negative perception.

This could easily damage his/her reputation and therefore cause harm to him/her professionally.

The area of context is one where you, as broadcaster, need to take great care. Even if what you're saying is intended as humour, the impact of your words could see you on the wrong side of law.

If You Can't Prove It, Don't Say It!

One of the most important points is to make absolutely sure that what you are saying is 100% true.

Do not make claims or accusations that you cannot prove in court.

Even if you think you can prove it, still be very cautious as proving things in court can be very difficult indeed.

You'll have to prove things with robust documentary evidence or first-hand corroboration from one or more people willing to testify in court.

Therefore, it's essential you make sure you get your facts right before you open the microphone.

Defences to a Libel Action

There are four main defences to libel:

> **Justification** — The matter is true both in substance and in fact. Remember, though, the burden of proof is on you. If the substance is sufficiently true, a court may overlook minor details of fact

> **Honest comment** — If the remarks are statements of opinion rather than fact, then it's an acceptable defence to say that the comment was made in good faith, without malice and on a matter of public concern.

> **Privilege** — This is a complex legal defence based on public interest, which applies to parliament and court hearings. Absolute Privilege covers what MPs say in Parliament and what people say in court. Qualified Privilege protects accurate and fair reports of those proceedings.

> **Live Broadcast** — You are partially protected if you were live on-air, took all reasonable precautions to ensure a libel didn't happen, had no reason to suspect it would and had no effective control over the speaker.

It's worth noting that you can't libel people who are dead.

What a Libel Has to Prove

In order for a libel action to succeed, someone ONLY has to prove:

> The statement is defamatory

> The statement refers to them

> The statement was broadcast/published

They DO NOT have to prove:

> The statement is false — the burden of proof is on the broadcaster/publisher

> The statement did any real damage — it's sufficient that it simply discredits someone

Part 2

CONTEMPT OF COURT

. . .

The Right to a Fair Trial

What Is Contempt of Court?

Contempt of Court is about protecting people's right to a fair trial.

It is separate to libel but equally as important, especially to radio presenters.

You become guilty of contempt when you broadcast material that creates a SUBSTANTIAL RISK of SERIOUS PREJUDICE to active legal proceedings such as an ongoing court case, regardless of your intent.

It becomes relevant or active from **the moment** anyone is arrested, charged or a warrant issued for their arrest.

Contempt can happen if a presenter, guest or caller passes their own judgment on a pending or current court case or broadcasts information which may prejudice jurors — like revealing a defendant's previous convictions for example.

A presenter's opinion (based on what he/she may have read in the paper, seen on TV or heard in news bulletins) could easily colour the view of a juror and/or allow the defendant to claim that he/she will be unable to receive a fair trial and therefore could walk free!

Consequences of Committing Contempt

Unlike libel which is a CIVIL matter and settled with the award of damages and apologies, contempt of court is a CRIMINAL matter.

This means it carries serious penalties and punishments. You and your boss could actually be imprisoned for something you say on the radio.

If you commit contempt, a judge can issue a summons for you to appear in court and you can be arrested.

A contempt case is usually only closed once you or your boss has "purged their contempt", in other words sincerely apologised in open court before a judge.

The best advice here is **NEVER EVER** discuss or comment on an ongoing trial or pending court case.

You should also ensure you don't comment on someone after they've been arrested or a warrant has been issued for their arrest.

The reporting of trials in news bulletins should always be handled with the utmost of care by trained journalists only.

Two Examples of Contempt on Radio

Rock FM

Two drive-time presenters at Rock FM in Preston, Mark Kaye and Judith Vause, were arrested and taken to court for something they said during the trial of Dr Harold Shipman in 2000.

The incident was considered so serious because jurors might have heard what the presenters said on their way home from the trial (which was taking place at Preston Crown Court), thus potentially prejudicing the case.

It could have led to the abandonment of the trial costing taxpayers hundreds of thousands of pounds.

Rock FM's boss, Michelle Surrell, had to "purge the contempt" by sincerely apologising to the court and the judge.

Rock FM Comments on Active Case

BBC NEWS

Monday, 9 April, 2001, 16:24 GMT 17:24 UK

Q&A: Journalists in contempt

The jury in the case of two Leeds United footballers accused of attacking a student was discharged following the publication of a "prejudicial" newspaper article.

BBC News Online asks:
How can journalists be in contempt of court?

Journalists are severely restricted in what they can report about a trial or criminal investigation once a case is "active".

When a warrant is issued for a suspect, an arrest is made or charges are brought, reporters must be careful not to publish or broadcast anything which poses a "substantial risk" of seriously prejudicing a fair trial.

What is prejudicial to a trial?

Though an ill-defined concept, roughly, news reports must not suggest the guilt of a person in custody or before the court. Such material could be argued to "prejudice" the deliberations of the jury.

For example, using the headline "Police arrest cat burglar" would land a reporter in hot water. "Man arrested in cat burglar case" would not.

Spicing up news reports with tales of a defendant's past behaviour (including any former convictions) will also probably result in contempt proceedings.

While journalists have a duty to openly report court proceedings, they must also take care not to mention any legal arguments made while the jury has been sent out or any evidence which has been deemed inadmissible.

So what is a "substantial" risk?

As with much legal language, what constitutes a "substantial" risk (according to the Contempt of Court Act of 1981) is open to debate.

In 1983 the Lord Chief Justice, Lord Lane, said: "A slight risk of serious prejudice is not enough, nor is a substantial risk of slight prejudice."

A questionable story hidden deep inside a newspaper is less likely to anger the court than a front page splash.

Likewise, a story in a local paper circulated in a region far from the court (and unlikely to be read by jurors) will not be as harshly treated as a report by a national publication.

Can pictures be in contempt?

When the question of a defendant's identity is central to a case, publications and broadcasters must avoid using their picture. A court might decide witnesses asked to link the defendant to the scene of the crime were influenced by images in the media.

What are the penalties?

In the Dr Harold Shipman trial, the judge hauled in a local radio manager and warned that two presenters had narrowly escaped a prison sentence for contempt of court.

Before the jury reached its verdict, Mark Kaye of Preston-based Rock FM complained about the high cost of the trial and added that Shipman was "innocent until proved guilty as sin", to a chorus of "guilty, guilty" from colleague Judith Vause.

In 1997, the Evening Standard was fined £40,000 (plus £50,000 legal costs) for revealing that three of the six men on trial for an escape from Whitemoor Prison were convicted IRA terrorists.

Do other countries share our contempt laws?

Even within the UK, contempt laws vary. For instance, Scottish reporters are renowned for being more scrupulous than their colleagues across the border.

In the United States there are no contempt laws as such.

How has the internet changed contempt laws?

Judges, lawyers and journalists are still struggling to work out how to accommodate the net into their understanding of contempt.

While a newspaper report usually ends up in the bin, online news archives often hold vast amounts of information (written about a person before their case became active) which could potentially prejudice a trial.

If such material represents a "substantial risk" has yet to be decided, but some defence lawyers are beginning to argue online archives do prejudice fair trials.

That the internet allows Britons easy access to foreign-based media outlets (which are not subject to our contempt laws) may also create headaches for the courts in the future.

This story from the BBC website highlights how the two Rock FM presenters almost faced a prison sentence for commenting on an active court case that was happening inside their transmission area.

Source: BBC Website
http://news.bbc.co.uk/1/hi/uk/1268966.stm

Beacon FM

The breakfast team at Beacon FM, Mark Peters and Lisa Freame, were removed from their show when they opened the phone lines to discuss the trial of Soham murderer Ian Huntley in 2003.

To make matters worse, the presenters even passed their own opinion on the case which was ongoing at the time.

Although they lost their jobs, neither they or the radio station were prosecuted for contempt because the trial was taking place at the Old Bailey in London, well away from their broadcast area of Telford in Shropshire.

This means what they said was unlikely to have prejudiced the jury because they would have been unable to hear it.

Of course, these days that would not apply as almost every radio station is streamed online and available to hear anywhere in the world.

Beacon FM Presenters Leave After On-Air Comments

BBC NEWS

Last Updated: Wednesday, 24 December, 2003, 11:25 GMT

✉ E-mail this to a friend   🖨 Printable version

DJs leave after Soham comments

Two local radio presenters whose comments during the Soham trial caused them to be investigated by the attorney general have left the station they worked for.

Mark Peters and Lisa Freame asked listeners of Beacon FM in the West Midlands whether Ian Huntley's testimony could be believed as they hosted a breakfast show phone-in.

Ian Huntley was convicted of the murders of the schoolgirls

The broadcast on 26 November appeared to breach the strict rules of court reporting, which ban any comment on the guilt or innocence of a person on trial.

At one point Mr Peters called into question Huntley's account of how Holly Wells and Jessica Chapman died in his house, saying: "It's almost like the most unbelievably made-up story in the world ever, really, isn't it?"

He added: "Well, I personally think it is.

"I can't believe any member of the jury is going to believe that story."

> 66 Do you idiots not understand the principle of sub judice? 99
>
> A listener's response to the broadcast

He and Ms Freame went on to encourage listeners to get in touch with the station with their comments.

Several listeners did contact the presenters to point out their apparent error.

'Opportunities elsewhere'

One texted the programme to say: "Do you idiots not understand the principle of sub judice?

"You can't comment on the trial.

"It's against the law. You're in a LOT of trouble!"

Radio Group GWR, the owner of Beacon FM, said on Wednesday that the presenters had left the station, which broadcasts to Shropshire and Wolverhampton.

A statement issued by the group said: "Following discussions between Beacon FM and Mark Peters and Lisa Freame, Beacon FM announces that Mark and Lisa will be leaving to pursue opportunities elsewhere."

Ruling awaited

Mr Peters and Ms Freame have not been on air since the broadcast.

A spokeswoman for the company said GWR had nothing more to say about the matter, and confirmed Nigel Freshman would host Beacon FM's breakfast show for the time being.

Attorney General Lord Goldsmith is still to make a ruling about whether the station and the two presenters will be prosecuted.

The pair could be fined or sent to prison if they are found guilty of contempt of court.

Commenting on an active trial is against the law and the consequences can be severe. This story shows the decisive action that needed to be taken by the radio station to limit the damage caused by on-air remarks during an active trial.

Source: BBC Website
http://news.bbc.co.uk/1/hi/england/shropshire/3346093.stm

More Things to Avoid Saying or Doing On-Air

> Revealing a previous conviction (or convictions)

> Saying someone has confessed or admitted the crime when they haven't

> Accusing somebody of a more serious crime

> Revealing prosecution evidence before the trial gets underway

> Derogatory comments suggesting a motive

> Comment about character related to the issue at the trial

> Saying whether you believe they are innocent or guilty

> Seeking or revealing jury deliberations

Why Do Newspapers 'Get Away With' Contempt?

Many broadcasters question why tabloid newspapers avoid prosecution for obviously ignoring the law by publishing details after someone has been arrested.

They rely on a defence known as the 'fade factor', that is the gap between publication and trial which can often be up to 10 months.

The longer the gap, the less the "substantial risk of serious prejudice" of the jury.

However when someone is arrested and subsequently released after questioning without charge, newspapers can find themselves at risk of libel action.

Chris Jefferies, a 65-year-old retired schoolteacher, was arrested after the murder of Jo Yeates in Bristol in 2010. Immediately after his arrest, tabloid newspapers described him variously as "strange", "weird", "lewd", "creepy", "a stalker" and linked him to previous paedophile and murder cases. He was released after questioning and never charged.

Not only did he accept substantial libel damages and apologies from eight newspapers but two of them were also successfully prosecuted for Contempt of Court and fined £18,000 and £50,000.

Conclusion

Failure to understand your legal responsibilities can cost you and your radio station lots of money. You could lose your job and possibly even end up inside a prison cell. And all of this would lead to bad publicity for you and your station.

Don't risk it — always take great care with your content.

The ultimate defence? **Don't say it in the first place!**

The laws of libel and contempt are complex and do change from time to time. So it's good practice to keep yourself up-to-date on any changes to the law.

If you are to be sued, **seek specialized legal help immediately.**

If you feel that you are unlikely to win the case, you should also think seriously about making an offer of amends or, if advised to do so by your representative, issue an apology.

The best advice:

If in doubt, leave it out.

About the Authors

PAUL HOLLINS is a radio presenter who has been on-air in most of the major markets in the UK. He started his career at Key 103 Manchester before working at BRMB in Birmingham, Capital FM London and London's Heart 106.2. In 1999 he set-up the radio content and syndication company Blue Revolution which is now one of Europe's largest providers of programming and radio services.

You can contact Paul Hollins at Blue Revolution
paul@bluerevolution.com
www.bluerevolution.com

PAUL CHANTLER has spent 25 years in the industry as a journalist, presenter, producer and programme executive. He was Group Programme Director at three of the UK's biggest radio groups in the 1990s and over the last ten years has built a highly successful international radio consultancy company with clients in the UK, Ireland, Europe and India. He is co-author of the book Essential Radio Journalism, originally published 20 years ago.

You can contact Paul Chantler at United Radio
paul.chantler@unitedradio.co.uk
www.unitedradio.com

Resources and Further Reading

Legal Training Seminars from United Radio Consultants
Contact: Paul Chantler, www.unitedradio.co.uk

**Essential Radio Journalism —
How to Produce and Present Radio News**
by Paul Chantler and Peter Stewart,
published by A&C Black, London.
Available from: www.radiobookshop.com/radiojournalism

Essential Law for Journalists
by Tom Welsh, Walter Greenwood and David Banks,
published by Oxford University Press.
Available from: www.radiobookshop.com/essentiallaw

Printed in Great Britain
by Amazon.co.uk, Ltd.,
Marston Gate.